MW00980855

To my Aunty 'Apple Cheeks'...may that onion booty turn heads in heaven...

Introduction

Life doesn't usually wait for a 2-week vacation to decompress, sit on the beach, drink daiquiris and gather our thoughts. Issues, problems and disappointments head our way every day, but so do moments of joy, exuberance and elation. It's our job to sort through all of the noise and get to the nitty gritty of our internal selves. 'Soul Work' is a tool to help you sort through your emotions and get to the heart of what is going on with you.

These journal prompts are meant to start the conversation with the most important person in your life...you. They are not to be answered quickly or in haste. Answer one question or spend a day on an entire chapter. Grab a notebook, find a quiet corner of the house, close the door to your office or steal away to the stock room at your job and start sifting through our soul. You may discover, as I often times do, that the problem you *think* you're having isn't really the issue at all. There was/is a problem that you have yet to deal with from your **past** that is rearing its ugly head in the **present**. Find a chapter that seems applicable to your situation and let it lead you. Cry it out. Laugh it out. Scream it out. Wherever you find yourself going, it's only for your benefit...

Dionne

Index:

ANGER/ FRUSTRATION/ SADNESS

Anger/Frustration/Sadness

1. Am I angry, happy, sad, anxious, nervous,

   excited?

2. Can I pin point when I started to feel this way?

3. Who did I feel good around today?

4. What did they say or do to make me feel

   good?

5. Would you like to spend more time around

   them?

6. Who did I feel bad around today?

7. Do I interact with them on a daily basis?

8. How can I limit our interactions?

9. What safeguards can I put around my life to

   protect myself from these type of people?

10. When was I my most sad, anxious, annoyed

    today?

11. What can I do to be less sad, anxious and

    annoyed?

12. When was I my most happy, hopeful, relaxed

    today?

13. What can I do to be more happy, hopeful and

    relaxed today?

14. Did I react in anger today?

15. Who/what was the trigger for my anger today?

16. Did I react in joy today?

17. Who/what was the trigger for my joy?

18. Was I stressed out today?

19. What mechanisms can I use to be less stressed?

ANXIETY

<u>Anxiety</u>

1. When was I my most anxious/stressed today?

2. What can I do to be less anxious/stressed?

3. Did I act out in anxiety today?

4. Who/what was the trigger for my anxiety?

5. I am anxious about _____

6. I'd be less anxious if _____

7. I get anxious around _____

8. I'm calm around _____

9. Do I have control of my time?

10. Does time manage me?

11. In what ways can I manage my time better?

12. Do I go to bed on time?

13. What do I think I'm missing when I go to bed

early?

14. How is staying up later benefiting me?

15. How is staying in bed later benefiting me?

16. What can I get done if I go to bed an hour

earlier?

17. What can I get done if I go to bed 2 hours

earlier?

18. What can I get done if I get up an hour earlier?

19. What can I get done if I get up 2 hours earlier?

20. Am I control of my finances?

21. Do I keep a budget?

22. Do I stay on my budget?

23. When am I most susceptible to overspending?

24. Who can I be accountable to help with my

    finances?

25. Am in control of my health?

26. When am I most susceptible to overeating?

27. Who can I be accountable to help with my

    eating habits?

28. Am I drinking too much?

29. How often do I think about drinking?

30. When am I most susceptible to drinking too

much?

31. What is my drug of choice (i.e. food, alcohol,

shopping, social media, significant other, etc...)

CAREER

Career

1. My dream career is _____

2. Am I working in my dream career?

3. What is the salary for my dream career?

4. Is that salary satisfactory for me?

5. How can supplement my income while pursuing

   my dream career?

6. What steps can I take to start working in my

   dream career?

7. Will my dream career require additional

   training?

8. What school has the courses I need to pursue

   my dream career?

9. Is there someone I can apprentice who is

   working in my dream career?

10. Have I reached out to someone in my dream

    career?

11. Do they have a coaching program?

12. Can I work in my dream career in my

    city/town?

13. Will I have to move to pursue my dream

    career?

14. Where is my dream career thriving?

15. How much will it cost to move to pursue my

dream career?

16. Are any of my friends working in my dream

career?

17. What type of friends do I need in order to get to

my dream career?

18. What friends will I need to let go of to pursue my

dream career?

CASTING CARES

Casting cares

1. What am I worried about today?

2. Is the issue I'm worried about fixable?

3. Can the issue I'm worried about be fixed by

   me?

4. Who can I reach out to help me fix the issue?

5. Am I ashamed to ask for help fixing the issue?

6. Why am I ashamed about the issue?

7. What will happen if I reach out for help to fix the

   issue?

8. Am I worried, scared, anxious, fearful?

9. What are the steps to resolve these cares?

10. Who can I call to discuss my issues?

11. What professional can help me manage my

    emotions?

12. Today I my release my anger for _____

    (can be a person, place or thing)

13. Today I release my fear about _____

14. Today I forgive myself for _____

15. Today I will make amends with _____

    (can be yourself)

16. What's one behavior I want to change today?

17. What's a positive action I can take to get back

on track with my goals?

FEAR

Fear

1. I'm afraid of _____ happening

2. Has this happened to me before?

3. What was the outcome?

4. Is this a rational fear?

5. What is the likelihood of this happening to me?

6. Has this thing happened to anyone I know?

7. What was the outcome?

8. Is it a fear of "it" happening or the outcome?

9. How did this fear come about?

10. Today I release my fear about/of _____

11. What is one thing I can do to get over this fear?

12. Who can I partner up with to get over this fear?

13. What would happen if this fear came true?

14. Would I be able to recover?

15. Is anyone I hang around fearful?

16. How much news do I watch?

17. What would happen if I didn't watch the news?

18. How much time do I spend on social media?

19. What would happen if I logged out of my social

   media?

20. What would happen if I deleted my social

   media accounts?

FINANCES

Finances

1. I feel _____ about my finances

2. I would feel less/more _____ about my

   finances if _____

3. I can bring in more money by _____

4. How much money do my friends make?

5. Am I the smartest person in my friend-circle?

6. Who's smart about money in my friend-circle?

7. Who in my friend-circle is wealthy?

8. Who in my friend-circle is always in financial

   trouble?

9. Do you talk to your friends about your finances?

10. Do you attend financial talks with your friends?

11. Would I like to make more money?

12. Would I like to invest in the stock market?

13. Would I like to start my own business?

14. Would I like to find an investor?

15. Do I have a financial planner?

16. Am I ashamed about my financial situation?

17. When is the last time I checked my credit

score?

18. Do I know who I owe money to?

19. How much do I owe on my debt?

20. How much do I have in my savings?

21. Do I budget my money each

    day/week/month?

22. I can decrease my debt by _____

23. I can increase my income by _____

24. I can increase my savings by _____

25. I can increase my giving by _____

26. How much money do I need to make a week

    to be content?

27. How much money do I need to make a month

   to be content?

28. How much money do I need to make a month

   to be content?

29. What car do I desire to drive?

30. What type of housing do I desire to live in?

31. What steps am I taking to live the way I want to

   live?

FORGIVENESS/ SHAME

Forgiveness/Shame

1. How was I nice to myself today?

2. How was I mean to myself today?

3. Was I impatient, disloyal and unkind with myself

   today?

4. Was I patient, loyal and kind to myself today?

5. I am angry at _____

6. I am angry because _____

7. I am hurt because _____

8. I am disappointed because _____

9. I am ashamed about _____

10. I am regretful about _____

11. I am in denial about _____

12. I am unhappy with _____

13. Today I my release my anger towards

_____ (can be a person, place or thing)

14. Today I forgive myself for _____

15. Today I let go of shame about _____

16. Today I let go of regret about _____

17. Today I will make amends with _____ (can

be yourself)

GRATITUDE

_____

Gratitude

1. How am I feeling in my physical body?

2. What aspect of my health am I thankful for?

3. What changes can I make in my physical body to be healthier?

4. What changes can I make in my self-care to have a healthier mind?

5. Is my family safe from harm?

6. Is my home safe from harm?

7. Is my automobile operable?

8. Is my business dwelling safe?

9. Did I receive any emergency calls today? If so, have they been resolved?

10. Is public transport operational?

11. How is the weather outside?

12. Am I employed?

13. What business can I start to be a blessing to someone?

14. What possessions am I grateful for today?

15. How can I share my possessions with others?

16. What tasks did I accomplish today?

17. What words of kindness to I speak to myself

today?

18. With whom can I share my abundance today?

19. What can I give away today?

20. With whom can I share my experiences with

today?

21. Who can I love on today?

22. Who loved on me today?

23. Who can I call and check on today?

24. Did I try anything new today?

25. What were my successes today?

26. Did I achieve any part of a goal today?

27. What one thing did I do well today?

28. Was I kind, gracious, complimentary today?

29. Did I compliment myself today?

30. What was "good" about today?

HAPPINESS

Happiness

1. I am excited about _____

2. I am hopeful about _____

3. I am joyful about _____

4. I am looking forward to _____

5. I am dreaming about _____

6. I am dreaming of a day when I can

    _____

7. What is one way I can bring more joy into my

    life?

8. What is one thing I can do today to be more

   joyful?

9. I'm most excited when I _____

10. How can I do more of the thing that make me

   excited?

11. Does the thing/s that excite me cost money?

12. How much money can I dedicate to do that

   thing that brings me the most joy?

13. How much time will I dedicate to the thing that

   makes me happy?

14. Are there any groups or organizations that like

    to do the same thing?

15. Do I know anyone that likes to do the same

    thing?

16. How can I spend more time with them?

MAKING

CHANGE

Making Change

1. What's one behavior I want to change today?

2. How do I want this behavior to look in 30 days?

3. How do I want this behavior to look in 60 days?

4. How do I want this behavior to look in 90 days?

5. How do I want this behavior to look in 6

   months?

6. How do I want this behavior to look in a year?

7. What changes can I make in my life to make

   this change?

8. Who's help can I enlist to help me change this

   behavior?

9. Who do I need to let go of to make this change

   happen?

10. What behaviors are disruptive and destructive

   to this change?

11. What's a positive action I can take to get back

   on track with my goals?

Daily Affirmations

I hear from God daily.

I have a sound mind.

I make wise decisions.

God loves me.

All is well.

I attract abundance.

I am healthy.

My marriage is blessed.

My children are blessed.

I am safe.

CPSIA information can be obtained
at www.ICGtesting.com
Printed in the USA
LVHW112326150922
728530LV00005B/254

9 781387 543908